KENNETH COPELAND

THE BLESSING OF THE LORD

MAKES RICH AND HE ADDS NO SORROW WITH IT

PROVERBS 10:22

STUDY GUIDE

THE BLESSING of The LORD Makes Rich and He Adds No Sorrow With It
Proverbs 10:22
Study Guide

ISBN 978-1-60463-140-1   30-0073

17 16 15 14 13 12   7 6 5 4 3 2

© 2011 Kenneth Copeland

Kenneth Copeland Publications
Fort Worth, TX 76192-0001

For more information about Kenneth Copeland Ministries, visit kcm.org or call 1-800-600-7395 (inside the U.S.) or 1-817-852-6000 (outside the U.S.).

This study guide is offered as a companion to the book, *THE BLESSING of The LORD Makes Rich and He Adds No Sorrow With It,* and is designed to create an opportunity for pastors, church groups, families and individuals to engage in a more in-depth study of THE BLESSING.

Presented in a simple, chapter-by-chapter format, this practical resource guides you through THE BLESSING book using simple, fill-in-the-blank and thought-provoking reflection and discussion questions. At the end of each chapter, space is included to make notes and record your personal growth and decisions. Space is also provided at the end of the study guide for recording your own, targeted faith confessions. Additionally, there is an "Answer Key" at the back of the study guide.

THE BLESSING *of The LORD Makes Rich and He Adds No Sorrow With It,* which Brother Copeland considers the most important writing he has ever accomplished, captures all he has learned about God's BLESSING throughout his more than 43 years of ministry. It is his desire that this study guide serve as an effective resource to enable the Church to come into the full knowledge of THE BLESSING and to rise up and take its place as God's powerful force of faith and action in the earth.

We at Kenneth Copeland Ministries join our faith with yours for the manifestation of Ephesians 3:20 in your life, that you will be blessed beyond anything you can ask or think, according to the power that works in you.

Chapter 1

THE BLESSING: Love's Ultimate Gift

1. For the first time in his adult life, Brother Copeland found himself in the perfect will of God in what year and location? _____

2. What scripture was it that sent shock waves through Brother Copeland's spirit? _____

   "I am the seed of Abraham! I am the product of a blood-sworn oath, a covenant cut between God and His firstborn Son. The LORD Jesus Christ is my blood Brother!"

3. God has already revealed Himself to us in His WORD that there are _____ _____ we have not yet learned and there are _____ _____ we have not yet received. Remember the Bible says "from faith to faith" and "from glory to glory" (Romans 1:17; 2 Corinthians 3:18).

4. The one BLESSING God spoke over Adam and Eve in the Garden of Eden set forth God's will for all mankind. What is that BLESSING and the scripture reference?

   _____

   _____

   _____

   _____

   Through that one BLESSING, God bestowed on the family of man everything they would ever need to become all He had created them to be, and do all He had destined them to do.

Reflection/Discussion Questions:

What decision does this chapter prompt you to make?

_____

_____

_____

_____

_____

How does what you've learned affect and change your future life and ministry?

_____

_____

_____

_____

_____

List some steps you are going to take from what you just learned.

a. _____

_____

_____

b. _____

_____

_____

c. _____

_____

_____

Chapter 2

The One Thing Sin Couldn't Change

1. Without question sin did change some things, but the one thing it did not change is _____. One of the most basic facts of God's nature is that He is the same yesterday, today and forever. James 1:17 calls Him "the Father of lights, with whom is no variableness, neither shadow of turning."

2. The best way for us to understand God's will for mankind is to go back to the first thing He said about it. The surest method for us to find His plan for us today is going back to His _____ _____ found in _____. Those familiar verses are more than a biblical history lesson. They set the stage for everything we, as believers, will ever need to know. They give us the first glimpse of God's purpose and plan for our lives.

3. As Christians we know that the true God is the God of the Bible. The God in Genesis 1:1 is the One, Eternal, Triune God—The God and Father of our LORD Jesus Christ (Ephesians 1:3). But even those titles, though correct, fall short of identifying God. The Bible describes God in depth from Genesis to Revelation but, in the end, He can be summed up in three breathtaking, yet simple New Testament words: _____ _____ _____, found in _____.

4. The Old Testament makes the same declaration. It says God is _____ _____ _____, found in _____.

5. If the Bible means what it says (and it does!) light is more than just a quality God possesses. It is who He is. It is His very nature. Just as God is Love, God is _____. Both Old and New Testament scriptures confirm this by describing God's appearance in terms of fire, lightning or some other form of light.

6. Instead of making man from an original design, God used _____ as His pattern (Genesis 1:26-27). When God created man, He actually copied _____.

7. From before "the beginning" God has seen every born-again believer as made _____ in His _____. He still sees us that way today.

8. Throughout the ages, God has maintained the _____ _____ of us He had in His heart from the first. It's the same as when He said in Genesis 1:3, *Light be!...* He said, *"Man be in our image, after our likeness: ...and have dominion!"*

9. As a living, speaking spirit like God, man had the same power to speak that God Himself had. He was full of God's own faith and had the authority to speak creative, compassionate words and exercise _____ with them. Born of God's WORD and created in His exact likeness, man was _____ just like God is _____. The only difference between man and God was this: Unlike God, who is eternally sovereign and independent, man was _____ on God. In all other ways, God and man were so exactly alike that when the angels saw God and Adam together for the first time, they must have thought they were seeing _____.

10. Adam was the _____ and _____ of God Himself. He wasn't just a *little* like God, he was *exactly* like Him. He didn't contain a part of God, he contained everything God is. He was absolutely filled with God.

11. Those words of _____ marked the coronation of mankind. They were the first words Adam ever heard (Genesis 1:28).

Reflection/Discussion Questions:

What decision does this chapter prompt you to make?

_____

_____

_____

_____

_____

How does what you've learned affect and change your future life and ministry?

_____

_____

_____

_____

_____

List some steps you are going to take from what you just learned.

a. _____

_____

_____

b. _____

_____

_____

c. _____

_____

_____

Chapter 3

Project Eden: Filling the Earth With the Glory of God

1. The word _____ has been so stripped of its meaning that most people pay no attention to it anymore, even though it represents the most important concept in the Bible and reveals God's will for all mankind.

2. The word _____ has a definite and distinct identity. Its primary biblical meaning is "to say something good about." In Hebrew, a *blessing* is the exact opposite of a _____, which means to say something bad about. The Jews, who were the original readers of the Bible, completely understood that fact. They never got blessings and curses mixed up. They knew: If it's good, it's a *BLESSING*. If it's bad, it's a *curse*.

3. The Hebrew definition of the word _____ gives us further proof that a blessing is a purely positive thing. It includes: "beautiful, best, better, bountiful, joyful, kindly, loving, merry, pleasant, prosperity, sweet, wealth and to be well." But there's another meaning for the word *blessing* that's even more exciting. It's a definition that comes into play when _____ gets involved.

4. When He is the One speaking, a BLESSING is defined as not only saying something good about someone, but as a *declaration which* _____ _____ _____ _____. Because God's words carry _____ _____ (as seen throughout Genesis 1) His BLESSING does more than express a positive sentiment. It releases the power to bring that BLESSING to pass. That's the reason THE BLESSING God spoke over mankind in Genesis 1:28 is so significant. God's declaration actually *empowered* man to prosper.

5. In Hebrew, the phrase *be fruitful, and multiply* means to increase and have _____ in every way. _____ means to fill up, to perpetually renew, supply and keep full. When God spoke those words, He endowed mankind with the divine power to increase and excel in everything good. He empowered them to fill the earth with that _____.

6. Through THE BLESSING, He said: *Prosper and fill this planet with My glory! Finish what I've*

   _____ _____. *Fill this place up with Me. Fill it up with compassion. Fill it up with love*

   and life, faith and holiness, and everything good!

7. God could have done the job Himself. He could have turned the whole planet into a Garden of Eden in an

   hour, but He had something else in mind. He wanted it to be a "_____ _____"—to watch

   His sons and daughters become His co-creators and finish out the planet. So He gave them the Garden of

   Eden as a pilot project to get them started. God's plan was for them to expand it until the earth became the

   garden spot of the universe. Once earth was finished, they could go to work on the rest of the planets.

8. Jesus left no doubt about man's _____ over the earth.

9. To see how important it is to be equipped for dominion, consider how Jesus transferred His authority

   to His disciples after His death and resurrection. He did it in two parts. First, He gave them the

   _____ _____ and told them what to do. Then, He equipped and empowered them through

   the power of the _____ _____ (Matthew 28:18-20). He said to them, "Ye shall receive

   power, after that the Holy Ghost is come upon you" (Acts 1:8).

10. THE BLESSING was Adam's divine mandate. It delivered to him both the _____ and the

    _____ to fill the earth with God's goodness. THE BLESSING does the same for us.

11. Brother Copeland learned that to operate in _____ _____, you just speak _____

    _____. Say about things what God says about them. Then, just go about your business and

    expect those things to come to pass.

12. God rested—not because He was tired but because He was finished. He had completed His work on the

    universe, poured Himself into mankind, crowned them with His creative power, and gave them total

    authority over the _____. There was nothing more for Him to do.

Reflection/Discussion Questions:

What decision does this chapter prompt you to make?

_____

_____

_____

_____

_____

How does what you've learned affect and change your future life and ministry?

_____

_____

_____

_____

_____

List some steps you are going to take from what you just learned.

a. _____

_____

_____

b. _____

_____

_____

c. _____

_____

_____

Chapter 4

The Day the Light Went Out

1. The Lord spoke to Brother Copeland in a voice that, on the inside of him, was audible and said, *Kenneth, if it hadn't been for _____, I never would have had a serious thought.* That statement came as a shock to him. It so contradicted the traditional concept of God, that he wasn't sure if he should believe it. But the more he thought about it, the more sense it made. It dawned on him that according to the Bible, heaven is the place where God's will is done. And there isn't anything in heaven to be serious about. There's no bitterness there, no sorrow there, no danger, no death. In a place like that, you can just have fun all the time.

2. God's command in Genesis 2:17 has been misunderstood. However it happened, Eve got the idea that she wasn't even supposed to touch the tree. But that wasn't true. God had commanded them to _____ and _____ it just like they did the other trees in the Garden.

3. Instead of staying away from the tree, they should have given it extra attention. They should have been especially committed to caring for it because it belonged to God. It represented God's fatherhood and headship over mankind. That's why God placed that tree in the center of the Garden: because their _____ with Him was supposed to be at the center of their lives.

4. God intended His tree to be a place where He and His family could fellowship with each other. He meant for Adam and his wife, and ultimately their children and grandchildren, to harvest the fruit of it and bring it to Him as an act of obedience and a confirmation of their love for Him. God wanted them to have the time of their lives returning to Him the _____ of His tree and celebrating the fact that He was then, and is now, the _____ of THE BLESSING that was upon them.

5. If you're wondering how Brother Copeland knew this, he found it out by reading the rest of the Book. He found it out by studying what the Bible says about _____, which is the practice of bringing to God the _____ that belong to Him.

6. Throughout scriptural history, God's people have drawn near to Him and connected with His covenant

of BLESSING, through the tithe. That's why in Genesis 4 we find Abel bringing God the firstborn of his flock. Although Abel lived thousands of years before the Law was given, somehow, he learned to tithe. Who taught him? There's only one possible answer. It must have been his father, _____.

7. So, where did tithing begin? _____

8. Adam should have slammed the devil's face up against the tree of the knowledge of good and evil and said, "You see that tree? That's God's tree. Adam should have laughed in his face when he told them that God didn't want them to be like Him. He should have said, "Hey, we're already like God! Haven't you heard? He made us in _____ _____.

9. What could have been the solution to Adam's sin? He could have _____ and taken _____ for what happened. But he didn't. When God came looking for him in the Garden, instead of running to Him and confessing his sin he cowered behind the bushes and tried to cover up his _____.

10. The whole message of the Bible is that God still loved Adam and Eve, even in their fallen state— as He has _____ the whole world ever since. He loved them so much that He was willing to _____ Himself to save them from the spiritual death trap that had ensnared them. His immediate response was not to _____ mankind for what they had done, but to _____ them from it.

11. God didn't release the curse. Adam did, by putting THE BLESSING into the hands of the devil. THE BLESSING became the exact _____ of what God had created it to be. THE BLESSING became the curse.

12. If one man has that much power in his fallen state, how much power and authority do we, as believers, have? We have *all power and all authority*—because Jesus does, and we are in Him, and He in us. The devil doesn't want you to know it, but this is the truth: *There's nothing bigger in this universe than a _____ _____.*

13. God did for His beloved Adam and Eve what had to be done. Sacrificing an animal, He covered

their nakedness and shame by making them tunics of skin. Through that sacrifice, He established the first _____ _____. He atoned for their sin and made a way to retain some form of relationship with them. Then, in His great mercy, God ensured that mankind would not live eternally in this fallen state (Genesis 3:22-24).

14. Adam and Eve knew what they were missing. The splendor of God's glory and the realm of the spirit had once been as tangible and accessible to them as the material realm. Now that whole realm had vanished, and they found themselves trapped by darkness below the _____ _____.

15. What is the light line? It's the line that separates the spiritual realm from the material realm. It exists because the light God released on the first day of Creation functions on two different levels. The higher level constitutes the world of the _____, and the lower (or slower) level constitutes the physical world of _____ (Colossians 1:16).

16. Adam and Eve found themselves trapped below the light line and confined to the natural world. In the 6,000 years that have passed since then, people have become accustomed to that confinement. Many have even come to believe that the visible realm is all that exists. They deny any reality they can't perceive with their natural senses. But those of us who are _____ _____ children of God know differently because our re-created spirits are in constant contact with the heavenly realm. We may not be able to see that realm with our natural eyes, but we can with the eye of _____.

Reflection/Discussion Questions:

What decision does this chapter prompt you to make?

_____

_____

_____

_____

_____

How does what you've learned affect and change your future life and ministry?

_____

_____

_____

_____

_____

List some steps you are going to take from what you just learned.

a. _____

_____

_____

b. _____

_____

_____

c. _____

_____

_____

Chapter 5

Activating Plan B: The Restoration Begins

1. God invoked Plan B. He bridged the gap between Himself and mankind by forging _____ _____ with those who would believe and honor Him. Through such men and women of faith, He preserved a _____ for Himself on the earth. He established a lineage that would eventually produce the devil-crushing Seed that He had spoken about in the Garden. He brought forth a covenant people through whom He could one day fully restore THE BLESSING.

2. Satan actually did have possession of the world's kingdoms and glory. That's why he was so determined to rid the planet of God's covenant bloodline. If he wanted to make his lordship over planet Earth permanent, he would have to destroy the ones through whom God intended to _____ _____ to all mankind. Every time he tried, however, he ran into one, major problem. He found that God Himself _____ His people.

God did not regret man's existence. He regretted that man was living on the earth under the curse instead of THE BLESSING (Genesis 6:5-8). Once the Flood was over and the tide of wickedness had been stemmed, mankind got a fresh start (Genesis 9:1-2).

3. If that BLESSING sounds familiar, it's because God said to Noah and his family the same thing He said to Adam in Genesis 1:28: _____ _____!

4. Since Noah and his sons—_____, _____ and _____—represented all the races and nations that would ever inhabit this planet, THE BLESSING could have been passed on through them to all the families of the earth.

5. Like Adam and Eve, however, Noah and his sons messed things up. Only Noah's first son, _____, stuck with God. So, it was through the bloodline of Shem that a man named

_____ was born. And it was through Abram—who would later be known as Abraham—that God made His next, mysterious move toward forever restoring THE BLESSING.

6. God was looking for someone who, by passing along his faith to his family, would perpetuate the lineage of THE BLESSING. He found that spark of faith in Abraham, and ignited that fire by saying the same thing to Abraham He'd said to _____. It was the same thing He'd said to Noah and his family. God declared to Abraham THE BLESSING. He empowered him to _____ and _____ in everything good and set him in the place of dominion by saying, "Whoever does good to you, I'll do good to them. Whoever comes against you, I'll come against them. I'll back you 100 percent" (Genesis 12:3).

7. God said, "In thee shall all families of the earth be _____." This is a vital point. For years, most Christians have not seen a connection between Adam's BLESSING and Abraham's BLESSING. Looking at the Bible as a collection of _____ _____, we've viewed scriptural history as if God were making it up as He went along. However, God's will for us is that we are BLESSED and He gave mankind THE BLESSING for all time. It will never change because God never changes.

8. The New Testament says that "the scripture, foreseeing that God would justify the heathen through faith, _preached before the gospel unto Abraham,_ saying, In thee shall all nations be BLESSED" (Galatians 3:8). According to those verses, Abraham heard the gospel the first time when God declared to him THE BLESSING in Genesis 12. But he didn't get the full impact of it until _____ ministered it to him. That's when he realized that through THE BLESSING, God was giving him possession, not just of the land of Canaan, but of the whole world.

9. As non-Hebrew-speaking Christians, most of us have never realized that's what Melchizedek said. We thought he was referring to God in Genesis 12 as possessor of heaven and earth. But, he wasn't. He was talking about God's covenant man. He was referring to "_____ of the Most High God" as possessor. If you have a hard time believing that, read Romans 4. It calls Abraham "the heir of the _____."

10. Brother Copeland had heard it preached that Melchizedek actually was _____, that he didn't have a mother or father, that he wasn't born and didn't die. But that's not true. Jewish history solves the mystery for us. He was Noah's son _____. What makes Melchizedek an Old Testament type

of _____ is the fact that he was anointed, both to declare THE BLESSING and to receive the

_____ (Hebrews 7:5-8). Any way you look at it—from the Garden of Eden on, THE BLESSING

and the _____ are connected.

Reflection/Discussion Questions:

What decision does this chapter prompt you to make?

_____

_____

_____

_____

How does what you've learned affect and change your future life and ministry?

_____

_____

_____

_____

List some steps you are going to take from what you just learned.

a. _____

_____

_____

b. _____

_____

_____

c. _____

_____

_____

Chapter 6

Tracking the Bloodline of THE BLESSING

1. Once Abraham locked his faith on to God's blood-sworn oath and believed, without wavering, that _____ _____ would bring forth a son for him and Sarah—despite that they were about _____ years old—_____ was born. Abraham raised his son just like God said he would. He taught him God's ways and trained him in the life and power of THE BLESSING. Of course, Isaac did more than just hear the stories. He lived some of them.

2. Hebrews 11:17-19 is what it means to be fully persuaded. Abraham knew that his God could and would do all that He had promised. That was Isaac's _____ _____ _____. He grew up seeing, hearing and believing that THE BLESSING always had and always would turn every situation in Abraham's favor. It's one thing to see THE BLESSING work for someone else. It's another thing altogether, to believe it will operate the same way for _____.

3. When Isaac heard those words (Genesis 26:2-5), the Almighty God appearing and speaking directly to him, his hair must have stood straight up. His knees went weak. His heart jumped right up into his throat. This was The LORD speaking to *him.* I believe, at that moment, the _____ hit Isaac like an 18-wheeler. *THE BLESSING of Abraham now belonged to him.*

4. Believers today need to catch that revelation the way Isaac did! We need to realize that every promise in the Bible is God's _____ _____ _____ to us. Because in Jesus, all His promises are yes and amen, God has said to us, just as surely as He said to Isaac, "I *WILL PERFORM* in your life THE BLESSING of Abraham. I _____you! I _____ you! I create the conditions of _____ around you, and you will carry _____ _____ to people everywhere you go!"

5. Through Isaac, THE BLESSING was passed down through the bloodline to his sons, _____ and _____. Had they both lived by faith in it, it would have produced the same results in their lives that it had for their father and grandfather. The elder one, Esau, thought so little of it that one day when he

was hungry, he traded it away for a bowl of stew. Just like _____, he gave up THE BLESSING for something to eat. God saw in Jacob a man who had faith in THE BLESSING (but no idea how to live in it).

6. God freely gave to _____ THE BLESSING he'd tried and failed to get by deception. He declared over him his blood-sworn inheritance; and Jacob responded—just as Abraham and Isaac had—by promising God the _____ (Genesis 28:13-15, 20-22).

7. With THE BLESSING activated in his life, Jacob expected things to start looking up—and in some ways, they did. There was just one problem, however. _____ was not an honest man. From the moment Jacob went to work for his uncle, Laban began cheating him. He made promises to Jacob and broke them. He defrauded him of his wages. But even so, _____ _____ kept working on Jacob's behalf.

8. Jacob didn't steal anything. He just lived by _____ in THE BLESSING and it kept increasing him until it absorbed everything they had. No longer was Jacob known as _The Deceiver_, but as Israel, _A Prince of God_.

Reflection/Discussion Questions:

What decision does this chapter prompt you to make?

_____

_____

_____

_____

_____

How does what you've learned affect and change your future life and ministry?

_____

_____

_____

_____

_____

List some steps you are going to take from what you just learned.

a. _____

_____

_____

b. _____

_____

_____

c. _____

_____

_____

Chapter 7

Ten Commandments of Love: Teaching the Israelites to Live in THE BLESSING

1. The tone of the Ten Commandments and the reason God gave them has been totally misunderstood through the years. People have assumed God gave them with a threatening voice and clenched fist. They've seen the commandments as _____, but nothing could be further from the truth. God gave those commands to Israel to teach them what _____, _____, _____ and _____ had once known. He wanted to teach them to live by faith in THE BLESSING. God's tone was not, "You had better do these things or else!" He was saying, "Here's how people who have a _____ with God conduct themselves."

2. When He said in the Ten Commandments "Thou shalt have no other gods before Me," He wasn't just being demanding. What was He telling them?

   _____

3. Every commandment was given in _____ because God is _____.

4. God wanted to renew the minds of the Israelites because whatever they carried on the inside would eventually come out. If they carried a mindset of bondage, they'd turn even the Promised Land into a place of bondage. But if they carried within them the mindset of BLESSING, that BLESSING would create a _____ ____ _____ wherever they went. Because we carry THE BLESSING inside us wherever we go, God can send us anywhere. And because of THE BLESSING that's within us, it can turn that dark corner of the world into a _____-and-_____ kind of place.

5. When God declared that BLESSING to Israel, He wasn't coming up with something new. He was simply telling them what was included in THE BLESSING they had inherited as the seed of _____. He was confirming to them the original _____—the one He had first released

on mankind in the Garden of Eden. That BLESSING is revealed in what book and chapter of the Bible?

_____

6. THE BLESSING works now just like it did back in Moses' day. If we'll take hold of the Ten

 Commandments by _____, they'll have the same effect on us they had on the _____

 who believed them. They'll cause us to excel and prosper wherever we live.

7. As New Covenant believers, we are not only protected from the curse, we have dominion over it. It has no

 authority over us unless we yield to it. Where do we find this in Scripture? _____

8. Where was Brother Copeland preaching when he experienced this truth firsthand? _____

 _____

9. Brother Copeland refused to sit in a wheelchair and walked all the way to the car with Gloria and his

 mother and father, who'd come to meet him at the plane. On the way home, he did something he'd never

 done before and has never done since. Where did Brother Copeland stay that night? _____

 _____

10. Brother Copeland went upstairs as soon as he got there and went to sleep—pain and all. He didn't

 know it, but after he fell asleep, his mother came and sat at the foot of the bed. She stayed there

 praying until about 2 a.m., when he sat straight up in bed and said, "_____ _____ _____

 _____!"

11. Sometimes, it takes that kind of _____ fight to walk in THE BLESSING. But it's a good

 _____ because it's a fight we win!

Reflection/Discussion Questions:

What decision does this chapter prompt you to make?

_____

_____

_____

_____

_____

How does what you've learned affect and change your future life and ministry?

_____

_____

_____

_____

_____

List some steps you are going to take from what you just learned.

a. _____

_____

_____

b. _____

_____

_____

c. _____

_____

_____

Chapter 8

The Day All Heaven Broke Loose

1. One day is with The LORD as a thousand years, and a thousand years as one day (2 Peter 3:8). So, for God, it was less than a _____ between the Garden of Eden and the birth of Jesus. How many days was it between the Garden of Eden and the birth of Jesus? _____

2. Despite the devil's feverish opposition, THE BLESSING always remained active through at least a _____. Throughout the ages, there was always a man or woman or group of stubborn believers who refused to let go of it.

3. True joy is a result of the inner working of the _____ _____. This comes from having God inside you. In those days, it was difficult to even imagine such a thing. But that wasn't all the angel of The LORD was telling them. _____ restored THE BLESSING to the whole human race. The angel was announcing to the sin-cursed human race that had fallen in the Garden of Eden and lived in a cursed world for 4,000 years, that the Garden was open once again.

4. _____ _____ is God's perfect will for humanity. _____ is the perfect will of God for humanity.

5. Even before Jesus had finished His mission on earth—before He went to the cross and completed the plan of redemption—God sent His angels to say, "Good news, everyone! _____ _____ is back!" That's how God always operates. He calls things that be _____ as though they _____ (Romans 4:17). He declares the end from the beginning. And, as always, the end He declared came to pass.

6. Every _____ Jesus performed and every work of ministry He accomplished on earth was a manifestation of THE BLESSING.

7. In places where the people believed it—like the area of Capernaum—THE BLESSING flowed like

a _____. People would follow Him around for days listening to Him teach, and multitudes would get healed. But in places like Nazareth, where people wouldn't _____, Jesus *could do no mighty work* (Mark 6:5). He wanted to—but couldn't because _____ slams the door on THE BLESSING.

8. The "Sermon on the Mount" is all about how to connect with and release the _____ of THE BLESSING!

Reflection/Discussion Questions:

What decision does this chapter prompt you to make?

_____

_____

_____

_____

_____

How does what you've learned affect and change your future life and ministry?

_____

_____

_____

_____

_____

List some steps you are going to take from what you just learned.

a. _____

_____

_____

b. _____

_____

_____

c. _____

_____

_____

Chapter 9

From the Cross to the Throne

1. God didn't send Jesus to be our example. He sent Him to be the _____ of a whole _____

   _____.

2. What the New Covenant _____ Jesus goes beyond what the natural mind can comprehend BUT

   He did it all to restore _____ _____.

3. Jesus is the second Person of the Godhead today. He didn't become something else when He ascended

   back into heaven. He is still a _____. He will forever be a man. He has the same body He had

   while ministering on earth. It's glorified now, of course. He proved that to Thomas after the Resurrection.

4. This is the startling truth of Christianity—that God's Son became a man forever and there is a resurrected,

   glorified man in the Trinity! He is the _____ of _____. He is the Victor of all, and He is

   our representative. We have been brought into the Godhead through Him.

5. Even after Jesus poured out the blood of the _____ _____, defeated the devil, released the

   captive saints and cleansed the heavenly utensils of worship from the contamination of Satan, wiping

   every trace of him out of heaven, Jesus wasn't quite finished with the work of _____. He had one

   more thing to do. He had to fulfill the promise He made to His disciples just before He went to the Cross

   (John 14:16). What was that promise? _____ _____

6. In Acts 2:2-4, what noise was made and why?

   _____ _____ _____ _____ _____

   _____ _____ _____ _____ _____

7. If you want your angels to spring into action, begin speaking _____ _____. Instead of talking sickness, poverty and defeat, confess _____ _____ over yourself. Say, "I'm BLESSED in the city. I'm BLESSED in the country. My body is BLESSED. My children are BLESSED. Everything I put my hand to prospers." Those are words the angels can go to work on. Those words will keep them busy doing good things for you.

8. God has assigned at least one angel (and probably more) to every _____.

Reflection/Discussion Questions:

What decision does this chapter prompt you to make?

_____

_____

_____

_____

_____

How does what you've learned affect and change your future life and ministry?

_____

_____

_____

_____

_____

List some steps you are going to take from what you just learned.

a. _____

_____

_____

b. _____

_____

_____

c. _____

_____

_____

Chapter 10

A Reborn Race

1. Most Christians don't know who they are. They have been _____ by the devil into believing they're "just old sinners saved by grace."

2. The phrase _____ _____ doesn't refer to something old that's been refurbished. It doesn't describe a forgiven sinner who's been cleaned up a little. A _____ _____ is a freshly created species of being that has never existed before; and that's what you are.

3. As New Testament believers, we have more than just a legal record of righteousness in heaven. We've actually been *made* the _____ of God in Christ, as spotless and without sin as Jesus Himself. To do that He had to make us *new creatures*.

4. The part of you that was re-created is your spirit—or what the Bible calls *the inner man* or *the hidden man of the heart*. Your spirit is the real you. In the Bible, it is often referred to as the _____ because it is the core of who you are. It's the life and power center of every human being.

5. Second Corinthians 3:18 describes the process best. It says that as we continue "to behold [in The WORD of God] as in a mirror the glory of The LORD, [we] are constantly being _____ into His very own image in ever increasing splendor and from one degree of glory to another…" *(The Amplified Bible)*.

6. All who want to operate in the fullness of THE BLESSING must understand what really happened to us when we were saved. We need to realize that the Creator Himself—the Holy Spirit—hovered over us, planted the seed of God's _____ within us, and we were _____ reborn.

7. One of the best pictures of what happens to our spirits at the new birth is found in the Genesis account of the creation of Adam, when God breathed divine life into him by saying, "Man, be in our image, after our likeness; have dominion over all the earth and everything in it" (Genesis 2:7, 1:26). When that WORD went into Adam, he lit up with the very life of _____ _____. He was Love just like

God is Love. He was Light just like God is Light. If you looked at _____ and _____ standing together, you wouldn't be able to tell one from the other because they were both covered in the same fire.

8. It's thrilling to know the same thing happened to _____ when we were born again! The very Spirit of Almighty God breathed new life into us.

9. If you could look inside yourself at your spirit right now, you'd be absolutely stunned because what you'd see is all the attributes of God. You'd see love, joy, peace, patience, resurrection power and glory. You'd realize that just as you were born naturally with the physical _____ of your parents, you have been born again with the spiritual _____ of God.

10. You need to get to the point where you feel as if you were using profanity if you said, "I'm just an old sinner saved by grace." Develop a _____ _____ instead of a sin consciousness, and that's when you'll really start having fun with The LORD!

11. Brother Oral Roberts said to Brother Copeland, "I've never made a _____." What did he mean?

_____

12. Brother Roberts said, "Once _____ have committed your life to The LORD Jesus Christ, and are doing your best to follow His WORD and walk uprightly before Him, you may do something that turns out to be a mistake. You may make some slips, but always remember: You have been _____! You didn't set out to make a mistake. There is no _____ to them who are in Christ Jesus, who walk not after the flesh, but after the spirit. Receive your forgiveness and keep going!" Brother Copeland got happy when he heard that because up to that point he had always felt like *Mr.* _____. From then on, he was *Mr.* _____. If you're a born-again believer, so are you (Ephesians 1:3-4)!

13. We should be _____ on what the Bible says about who we are and _____ _____ that is on us.

14. Stand steadfastly on the fact that through the plan of redemption, Jesus has restored to you THE BLESSING *in its entirety.* Then put that BLESSING to work by _____. Let it start creating a _____ _____ in your home, your church, your business and your neighborhood.

Let it flow through you, out into the streets to others who need help.

15. As Jesus' disciples, we should be identifying with _____.

16. According to God's WORD, this whole planet belongs to you, me and every other believer. "The promise to Abraham and his posterity, that he should inherit the world" is _____ as _____ of THE BLESSING. Through Jesus, the last Adam, we have once again been given title deed to the earth. Through Him, mankind has gotten back the _____.

17. In Hebrews 4:3-4, 9-10, with THE BLESSING back in operation, we, as believers, don't have to toil, sweat and strain to *make a living* like people who are dependent on the ungodly system of this world. The earth doesn't fight us when we cultivate it, nor does it produce thorns and thistles and curse us every time we put our hand to it. That curse has been lifted from us! Because of what _____ did, we can enter into God's _____ and put THE BLESSING to work for us.

18. We can stop struggling along with our own strength and trust THE BLESSING to empower us to fulfill our original mission. What is that mission? The same as it's always been: to create the _____ _____ _____ wherever we go. How do we do it? We do that first by preaching the _____. And, by letting people know that through Him, the Garden of Eden is _____ again.

In West Virginia, the state has a new phrase "Open for Business." Because of Jesus, when we believe the message of faith and are born again, we realize the Garden of Eden is again open for business in our lives. What do we do then?

1. We preach about it.

2. We let people know the Garden of Eden is open.

3. We walk in THE BLESSING ourselves to give people an example to follow.

19. Someone might say, "I'm going to pray God will cast the devil out of my city and get everyone saved, healed and prosperous." Go ahead and pray that if you want to, but it won't do any good. Jesus never said He'd take the gospel to your town. He didn't say He'd cast the devil out of it. He didn't say He'd

lay hands on the people around you and heal them. He said, "_____ go into all the world and preach the gospel to every creature. _____ cast out demons. _____ lay hands on the sick and they'll recover. _____ go—and _____ go with you."

That's just another way of saying, "Exercise authority over the earth. Take dominion and subdue it. Take THE BLESSING around the globe, and fill the whole place with the glory of God." That commission isn't just for preachers. It's for every member of the Body of Christ. You ought to be acting on it. You ought to be saying every day when you get up, "I am BLESSED. THE BLESSING of Abraham is mine. Jesus has put it in me and on me; and that BLESSING is flowing out of my body."

Discuss the example of Guatemala that Brother Copeland gives in regard to the Garden of Eden being established in the world.

_____

_____

_____

_____

Reflection/Discussion Questions:

What decision does this chapter prompt you to make?

_____

_____

_____

_____

_____

How does what you've learned affect and change your future life and ministry?

_____

_____

_____

_____

_____

List some steps you are going to take from what you just learned.

a. _____

_____

_____

b. _____

_____

_____

c. _____

_____

_____

Chapter 11

The LORD and High Priest of
THE BLESSING

1. Jesus, as our _____ _____, is the Minister of THE BLESSING.

2. One aspect of THE BLESSING He ministers is _____ and _____. That, however, is not the end of the story. Jesus didn't just procure a pardon for us from our past transgressions or merely release us from the penalty of sin. He defeated the whole sin system. He released the law of the Spirit of life in us and made us free from the law of sin and death, completely destroying the power of sin and the devil.

3. The New Testament makes a clear distinction between Jesus' _____ and His _____ _____. Speaking of His post-resurrection exaltation, it says, "God hath made that same Jesus… *both Lord and Christ."*

4. The term *Christ,* which in Greek means "_____ _____ _____ and _____ _____," refers to Jesus' ministry as High Priest and Administrator of THE BLESSING. The term *Lord* refers to His position as _____, _____ and _____ _____ who put death under His feet. He is the One with the Name above all names at the sound of which, every knee bows and every tongue confesses in heaven, earth and under the earth, that Jesus Christ is Lord. He is Lord over sickness, poverty and everything in this world system that attempts to steal any portion of THE BLESSING from us. And, because we have been raised up and seated together with Him in heavenly places, we have both the right and responsibility to stand on that lordship by faith and resist the devil until he flees from us. That's what the Apostle Paul was telling us to do in what he wrote in Ephesians 6:10-13.

5. This passage reminds us that He _____ that responsibility to us by making *us* "kings and priests."

6. Once you know you're properly resisting the devil on the basis of God's _____, all you have to do to enforce the devil's defeat and run him out of any situation, is to maintain your _____

_____ _____.

"But sometimes I get tired when I have to stand a long time." You won't get tired at all if you do what those verses tell you to do. If you'll keep praying always...in the spirit, you'll get stronger by the minute because you're building yourself up on your most holy faith (Ephesians 6:14-18).

Always confess: "Greater is He that is in me than he that is in the world...." Also remember we exercise the power of life and death with our tongues. Psalm 91 helps us in our faith-covenant connection. When we speak The WORD of The LORD, He declares THE BLESSING over us. He says, "Yes, I will administer that confession." Can you see what a joy and thrill it is to know we're backed up by Jesus' high priestly ministry?

7. Abraham didn't just take that BLESSING and say, "Thank You. I appreciate that," and walk away. Both _____ and _____ tell us he responded to THE BLESSING in a very specific way, just as God had planned for Adam to respond to it in the Garden—by _____.

8. We ought to prayerfully and reverently bring our tithes to Jesus our High Priest and release our _____ every time, as a fresh expression of THE BLESSING.

9. Abraham understood far better than many Christians today just how significant that covenant interaction was. He knew the Communion elements, representing _____ covenant, meant that God was pledging His own life to him. He understood that God was swearing _____ _____ to him that would never be broken—He would cease to exist before He'd ever break His covenant with Abraham (Hebrews 6:16-20).

10. So instead of being led by our emotions, our soul should be _____ in THE BLESSING. At that point tithing becomes a privilege and a thrill because we're doing it in response to the fact that God has BLESSED us.

We have access to the limitless resources of heaven because we are living through Jesus as we read in 1 John 4:9.

11. We need to get this fact established in our thinking: Administering THE BLESSING isn't supposed to be _____. It's what we're born to do! If we'll just dare to believe that, we can have the time of our lives.

Reflection/Discussion Questions:

What decision does this chapter prompt you to make?

_____

_____

_____

_____

_____

How does what you've learned affect and change your future life and ministry?

_____

_____

_____

_____

_____

List some steps you are going to take from what you just learned.

a. _____

_____

_____

b. _____

_____

_____

c. _____

_____

Chapter 12

Following the Faith of Abraham

1. The first question that comes to mind once you grasp the awesome magnitude of THE BLESSING is this: *How do I get it to operate in my life?* That's something we all need to know. All those things became ours the moment we were _____ _____.

2. As _____ _____ with Jesus, we are—*right now*—co-possessors of everything in heaven and earth.

The Bible explains it to us with one short phrase in Galatians 3:14. Read and discuss.

_____

_____

_____

_____

3. The *faith* of Abraham is what originally activated THE BLESSING of Abraham, and it still does. That's why God said that "_____ _____ it is impossible to please him."

4. Although Brother Copeland is very much in favor of obeying God's commands, when someone just keeps rules without faith religion doesn't work. "Why, Brother Copeland, how can you say that? Christianity is a religion!" People made a religion out of it, but true Christianity is God and His _____—a family made up of people who are saved, made righteous and BLESSED *through faith,* that lives, not by a set of religious rules, but by the love of God and the same kind of faith Abraham had.

5. When Brother Copeland found out the Bible is a blood-covenant book, and the New Testament is actually the New Covenant in Jesus' blood, his faith in God skyrocketed. The more he found out what God had said to him in the book of His blood-sworn oath, the more Brother Copeland's ability to _____ ____ _____ and what He would do for Brother Copeland soared.

6. Brother Copeland made the _____ final authority in his life. That's the first step to unlocking its power. You must settle in your heart once and for all that you will believe and act on whatever it says. You must decide that from this point forward, instead of adjusting The WORD to fit your _____, you will adjust your lifestyle to fit The WORD.

7. As believers, we must have the same attitude toward the Bible if we want its power to be released in our lives. We must treat it as the _____ _____, believe every word of it, and operate accordingly. Then—and only then—will our lives begin to take off.

8. Once you've made a quality decision to make _____ _____ your _____ _____, the next step in the process of faith is to follow the instructions God gives us in Proverbs 4:20-22.

9. For The WORD to produce results in your life, you must give it _____ _____ by spending time studying it and meditating on it.

10. Some people think God just gave Brother Copeland the ability to live by faith because he's a preacher. They say he has some kind of special gift for it. But that's not true. The faith he has came by hearing… and hearing…and hearing The WORD of God. He likes to call the time he spends hearing and meditating on The WORD _____ _____, because it builds us up to a place of faith and gets us ready to step out on that WORD and release its creative power.

11. You don't have to understand it. All you have to do is believe it and act on it. If you'll do that, The WORD will _____ whether you understand how it works, or not. Jesus said so in the parable of the sower, where He referred to The WORD of God as a _____ (Mark 4).

12. Your spirit is created to process God's WORD and generate faith from it in much the same way your digestive system processes food and generates physical energy. When you read a promise in The WORD of God and say, "I believe I receive that," your _____ goes to work digesting that WORD and producing _____.

13. Our _____ produce our future. What we're saying today is what we'll have tomorrow. Like it or

not, we can't get around it. We live in a word-based, word-created, word-directed environment.

14. Abraham, the father of our faith, proved that beyond any shadow of a doubt. He kept building his faith until he got to the point where he was *fully persuaded*—despite every circumstance to the contrary—that he and his barren, old wife were going to have a baby. And he did it by walking out the process. What is the process? The process is _____ the _____ _____ _____ and then _____ on them.

15. Ephesians 5:1: "Therefore be imitators of God as dear children" *(New King James Version).* The word _____ used in that verse comes from the Greek word which means _____ _____. We're supposed to mimic God the way children mimic their parents.

One of Brother Copeland's friends, John Osteen, wrote a book titled, There's a Miracle in Your Mouth.

16. Discuss one of Brother Copeland's favorite stories having to do with speaking and acting.

_____

_____

_____

_____

17. At that moment, the Shunammite's circumstances didn't look BLESSED. Emotionally, she didn't feel BLESSED. But she _____ she was BLESSED. So she called things that be not as though they were, knelt down, grabbed Elisha's feet and refused to leave him until he agreed to go back with her and minister to her child.

Yes, there is a miracle in your mouth. Read Romans 10:8 and discuss.

_____

_____

_____

_____

18. You must decide that you are going to trust The WORD of God and must immerse in it, and build yourself up in faith. Then, there is an element that Brother Copeland calls The _____. When it's time for The Delivery, something happens in your spirit. On the outside, things may not look any better. The symptoms or circumstances you've been standing against may not have changed one bit. Yet, all of a sudden, almost without thinking about it, the _____ _____ _____ comes roaring out of your mouth with such power that you know you have the _____.

19. When things start to happen, it's exciting. But it's also a time when you must stay full of _____ that THE BLESSING is working in your life. You must continue to be patient and keep believing it's working—when you see it and when you don't, when you feel it and when you don't.

20. Discuss the example that Brother Copeland gives of the 1,520 acres of property that are now the headquarters of KCM. How many years were spent sowing and believing for it?

    _____

    _____

    _____

    _____

21. Create an inner image of God's WORD coming to pass and His BLESSING manifesting in your life. Bathe your imagination in The WORD of God until _____ rises up within you and begins to take upon itself _____.

Reflection/Discussion Questions:

What decision does this chapter prompt you to make?

_____

_____

_____

_____

_____

How does what you've learned affect and change your future life and ministry?

_____

_____

_____

_____

_____

List some steps you are going to take from what you just learned.

a. _____

_____

_____

b. _____

_____

_____

c. _____

_____

_____

Chapter 13

Breaking the Fear Connection

Everyone who has ever lived by faith in God's WORD and dared to encourage others to do so, eventually runs into someone who says, "I tried The WORD and it didn't work!" One friend of Brother Copeland's has a great answer for people like that. He says, "No, The WORD tried you, and you didn't work." Jeremiah 1:12 says, "I will hasten my WORD to perform it"; and that's what He does. Always. Without fail.

1. Fear _____ is faith _____. Jesus settled that issue by what He said in Mark 5 to a man named Jairus who came seeking healing for his dying child.

Discuss how Jairus' faith brought healing to his child.

_____

_____

_____

_____

2. Just as faith is the spirit connector to God and THE BLESSING, fear is the spirit connector to the devil and the curse. We've already seen throughout the Bible, _____ is what activates the operation of THE BLESSING. Faith releases the Anointing of God in people's lives. When Jesus ministered on earth, and preached *peace* (*shalom:* which includes healing, deliverance, prosperity, and a life with nothing missing and nothing broken), the people who believed what He preached connected with Him and received that peace.

3. Every manifestation of the _____ is a form of the devil's opposition.

4. Fear is the connector to sickness and disease, poverty and every other manifestation of the curse. According to Isaiah 10:27, the yoke (or oppression) of the devil is *destroyed* by the _____. So, Brother Copeland calls the anointing *the burden-removing, yoke-destroying power of God.*

THE BLESSING OF THE LORD STUDY GUIDE

The anointing destroys the yoke of oppression. It renders it unfit for Satan's use. If it were just broken, it could be mended. But, the anointing doesn't break it. It explodes it into powder.

5. Just as _____ _____ _____ connects to the Spirit of the anointing, fear connects to the spirit of the anti-anointing. We must come to the absolute, rock-solid, scriptural conviction that through the power of redemption, Jesus has delivered us once and for all from the bondage of _____.

Galatians 3:13 says it this way: "Christ hath redeemed us from the curse of the law, being made a curse for us: for it is written, Cursed is every one that hangeth on a tree."

6. Once you understand that Jesus has purchased your complete and absolute deliverance from fear, you're on your way to living fear free. You have a solid, scriptural basis from which to resist it. But that, in itself, won't totally get rid of it. What gets rid of it? _____

7. In the life of a believer, love starts with the revelation that _____ _____ _____ _____ _____ (1 John 4:10, 16-18).

We must get into our spirit that God Almighty loves us, just like He loves Jesus.

Affirm that God's own love equipment is inside you and every person who has ever made Jesus the Lord of their lives. It literally flushes fear out of our systems. As we activate love by receiving it from God, loving Him in return, and then loving our neighbor as ourselves, the tide of love keeps rising and rising until it sweeps fear away like a flood. That's the moment we can rebuke it, and it will leave us.

8. When your thoughts start going the wrong way, use your mouth to turn them in the _____ direction. Any negative, fearful thought you have can be subdued and overcome by speaking _____ _____. You can leave the devil helpless as a kitten by contradicting him with the words of your mouth and refusing to take his thoughts.

Discuss the story of Kellie when she was 4 years old and how she wouldn't take a thought. What are some ways in your life that your thoughts can change your circumstances?

_____

_____

_____

_____

You have been delivered from fear by the blood of Jesus and have the love of Almighty God Himself shed abroad in your heart. But, if you're wise, you won't wait until you're looking a serial killer in the face or dealing with a terrorist attack to develop yourself in those things. Don't wait until something bad happens and then start trying to train for it.

Reflection/Discussion Questions:

What decision does this chapter prompt you to make?

_____

_____

_____

_____

_____

How does what you've learned affect and change your future life and ministry?

_____

_____

_____

_____

_____

List some steps you are going to take from what you just learned.

a. _____

_____

_____

b. _____

_____

_____

c. _____

_____

_____

Chapter 14

The Royal Law of the Kingdom

1. To walk in THE BLESSING, everything must hang on _____.

2. Love is THE commandment of God because love is THE law that governs the operation of _____ _____.

A law that works right alongside the law of faith is found in Galatians 5:6: "faith...worketh by love." That is a practical, unalterable truth.

3. Everything that is contrary to Love goes against your very substance. Every word of disharmony violates the way you were made. Unloving words, thoughts and actions do violence to the very _____ and _____ in your physical body. Discuss how this impacts your life daily.

_____

_____

_____

_____

Jesus' command of love is nonnegotiable. Brother Copeland compares it to the general orders of the Army.

4. If there's something amiss between you and another believer, you must make the first move. Don't sit around waiting for him to apologize to you. Do your best to make _____ and put things right (Matthew 18:15-17).

5. Exercising _____ releases health and life. It's one of the most powerful things you can do to get the love and power of God flowing freely through you again. So take time often to do it. Discuss ways that you can apply this to your life today.

_____

_____

_____

_____

6. Everything in you is made of love. All God's mercy, goodness, kindness, love, joy, peace and meekness have been invested into your spirit. You have the same capacity to love that _____ has because His own love has been shed abroad in your heart by the Holy Ghost. What you must do is _____ that capacity by making _____ the priority of your life. You must decide that, first and foremost, you are a keeper of the _____ _____ _____.

7. To maintain that kind of spiritual strength, however, you must spend _____ _____ _____ _____. Spend time in His WORD and keep yourself filled with it. One church service a week will not do it. Your fellowship with The LORD must be _____.

8. THE BLESSING is continually working for you. You don't have to strive and sweat to make things turn out for yourself. You don't have to worry about a thing. All you have to do is keep the command of love and stand on the _____. Love, believe, obey…and you'll be BLESSED.

9. With every step of love we take, we're getting closer, and THE BLESSING is overtaking us more and more. What happens as it overtakes us? It begins to change things in our lives into a replica of the _____ _____ _____. It turns sickness into health and poverty into _____. All THE BLESSINGS of God come on us, and we begin to have "days of heaven upon the earth."

Reflection/Discussion Questions:

What decision does this chapter prompt you to make?

_____

_____

_____

_____

_____

How does what you've learned affect and change your future life and ministry?

_____

_____

_____

_____

_____

List some steps you are going to take from what you just learned.

a. _____

_____

_____

b. _____

_____

_____

c. _____

_____

_____

Chapter 15

Come Sit With Me

1. God has issued us an invitation that enables us to triumph over every test and trial the devil sends our way. He has said to us: "Sit thou at my right hand, until I make thine enemies thy footstool."

   "But I thought God said that to Jesus." He did. But it applies to us just as surely as it does to our resurrected Lord Himself because Jesus isn't sitting alone at God's right hand. _____ are sitting there with Him.

2. Why do some Christians approach God like beggars and plead for help, or struggle in their own strength to work things out? It's because the idea of sitting down and trusting God to take care of them seems presumptuous and irresponsible. "It would be asking too much to expect God to take care of everything for me. Surely, God expects me to do something!" They don't realize that what God expects us to do is sit down and enter His rest, and He is grieved when we don't do it. The book of _____ makes that very clear.

Discuss ways that you can sit with God and talk with Him.

_____

_____

_____

_____

3. Get up every morning thinking, *What is God going to do for me today?* Every time the phone rings, you think, *This is it! God is about to BLESS me again!* Brother Copeland has been living this way for decades now. It still excites him when the phone rings because he's always expecting. It's impossible to have that kind of fun when you are working for a living. What's more, no matter how hard you work, you can't earn the kind of wealth _____ _____ brings.

4. If you want to live in God's rest, you must continually declare _____ _____. You can't just sit there and be silent. _____ _____! So hold fast to your confession of faith. Sit down,

saying The WORD of God about your situation and nothing else. Sit down with praise on your lips and declare, "The LORD is my refuge and my fortress, my God, in Him will I trust."

Reflect on the story of Brother and Sister Copeland paying off someone's house.

_____

_____

_____

_____

5. If you're just getting started in this, you may not yet be at the place financially where you can pay off someone's house, but start where you are. BLESS people with your loving attitude. BLESS them with your smile. Buy someone's lunch. All the while, just keep putting your faith in _____ _____. Keep expecting it to increase you. Meditate on it and act on it until the reality of it revolutionizes your thinking, fuels your faith and sends you soaring into the heights of God's will for your life. Stay with it until, like the true seed of _____ that you are in _____ _____, you become a BLESSING to all the families of the earth!

Reflection/Discussion Questions:

What decision does this chapter prompt you to make?

_____

_____

_____

_____

_____

How does what you've learned affect and change your future life and ministry?

_____

_____

_____

_____

_____

List some steps you are going to take from what you just learned.

a. _____

_____

_____

b. _____

_____

_____

c. _____

_____

_____

Compile your list of next steps from each of the preceding chapters and write a faith confession for your future. Take action by affirming this confession each day and watch this confession come to pass.

_____

_____

_____

_____

_____

_____

_____

_____

_____

_____

_____

_____

_____

_____

_____

_____

_____

_____

_____

_____

KENNETH COPELAND

THE BLESSING

OF THE

LORD

MAKES RICH
AND HE ADDS
NO SORROW
WITH IT

PROVERBS 10:22

ANSWER KEY

CHAPTER 1

THE BLESSING: Love's Ultimate Gift

1. In 1966 in Tulsa, Okla. (pg. 20)

2. Galatians 3:9, We are "BLESSED with faithful Abraham." (pg. 20)

3. scriptural truths; biblical revelations (pg. 24)

4. Genesis 1:28, "Be fruitful, and multiply, and replenish the earth, and subdue it: and have dominion…."
   (pg. 27)

CHAPTER 2

The One Thing Sin Couldn't Change

1. God (pg. 32)

2. original plan; Genesis 1:1-3 (pg. 33)

3. God is love; 1 John 4:8 (pg. 34)

4. full of compassion; Psalm 78:38; 111:4 (pg. 34)

5. Light (pg. 39)

6. Himself; Himself (pg. 43)

7. perfectly; image (pg. 43)

8. inner image (pg. 44)

9. dominion; Love; Love; dependent; double (pg. 47)

10. spirit; image (pg. 48)

11. BLESSING (pg. 48)

CHAPTER 3

Project Eden: Filling the Earth With the Glory of God

1. blessing (pg. 49)

2. blessing; curse (pg. 50)

3. good; God (pg. 51)

4. empowers them to prosper; creative power (pg. 51)

5. abundance; Replenish; goodness (pg. 52)

6. started here (pg. 52)

7. family project (pg. 53)

8. authority (pg. 54)

9. Great Commission; Holy Ghost (pgs. 55-56)

10. responsibility; resources (pg. 57)

11. THE BLESSING; The WORD (pg. 60)

12. earth (pg. 63)

CHAPTER 4

The Day the Light Went Out

1. sin (pg. 68)

2. tend; keep (pg. 69)

3. relationship (pg. 70)

4. fruit; Source (pg. 70)

5. tithing; firstfruits (pg. 70)

6. Adam (pg. 70)

7. In the Garden of Eden (pg. 70)

8. His image (pg. 75)

9. repented; responsibility; shame (pg. 77)

10. loved; sacrifice; punish; redeem (pg. 78)

11. opposite (pg. 78)

12. redeemed man (pg. 81)

13. blood covenant (pg. 83)

14. light line (pg. 86)

15. spirit; matter (pg. 86)

16. born again; faith (pg. 88)

CHAPTER 5

Activating Plan B: The Restoration Begins

1. covenant relationships; bloodline (pg. 89)

2. restore dominion; defended (pg. 91)

3. Be BLESSED (pg. 94)

4. Shem; Ham; Japheth (pg. 94)

5. Shem; Abram (pgs. 94-95)

6. Adam; prosper; excel (pg. 95)

7. BLESSED; disjointed incidents (pg. 96)

8. Melchizedek (pg. 103)

9. Abram; world (pg. 103)

10. Jesus; Shem; Jesus; tithe; tithe (pgs. 104-105)

CHAPTER 6

Tracking the Bloodline of THE BLESSING

1. THE BLESSING; 100; Isaac (pg. 109)

2. heritage of faith; you (pg. 112)

3. revelation (pg. 113)

4. blood-sworn oath; heal; prosper; Eden; THE BLESSING (pg. 113)

5. Jacob; Esau; Adam (pgs. 114-115)

6. Jacob; tithe (pg. 116)

7. Laban; THE BLESSING (pg. 116)

8. faith (pg. 117)

CHAPTER 7

Ten Commandments of Love: Teaching the Israelites to Live in THE BLESSING

1. legalistic; Abraham; Isaac; Jacob; Joseph; covenant (pgs. 131-132)

2. He was the only God they would ever need (pg. 132)

3. love; love (pg. 133)

4. Garden of Eden; milk; honey (pg. 135)

5. Abraham; BLESSING; Deuteronomy 28 (pg. 138)

6. faith; Israelites (pg. 145)

7. Galatians 3:13-14 (pg. 146)

8. Shreveport, Louisiana (pg. 147)

9. He stayed with his parents (pg. 148)

10. Glory be to God (pg. 148)

11. faith; fight (pg. 148)

CHAPTER 8

The Day All Heaven Broke Loose

1. week; 4 days (4,000 years) (pg. 151)

2. remnant (pg. 152)

3. Holy Spirit; Jesus (pg. 154)

4. THE BLESSING; Jesus (pg. 155)

5. THE BLESSING; not; were (pg. 156)

6. miracle (pg. 156)

7. river; believe; unbelief (pg. 161)

8. power (pg. 163)

CHAPTER 9

From the Cross to the Throne

1. firstborn; new breed (pg. 166)

2. cost; THE BLESSING (pg. 167)

3. man (pg. 174)

4. Champion; champions (pg. 174)

5. New Covenant; redemption; Sending the Holy Spirit (pgs. 175-176)

6. Mighty wind; Roar of angels and the sound of THE BLESSING coming on the scene (pgs. 176-177)

7. The WORD; THE BLESSING (pg. 178)

8. believer (pg. 180)

CHAPTER 10

A Reborn Race

1. brainwashed (pg. 184)

2. new creature; new creature (pg. 185)

3. righteousness (pg. 186)

4. heart (pg. 186)

5. transfigured (pg. 187)

6. WORD; spiritually (pg. 188)

7. God Himself; God; Adam (pg. 188)

8. us (pg. 189)

9. DNA; genetics (pg. 189)

10. righteousness consciousness (pg. 190)

11. mistake; He's done a lot of things that turned out to be mistakes, but he never did get up in the morning and say, "I believe I'll make some mistakes today." (pgs. 191-192)

12. you; redeemed; condemnation; Mistake; Redeemed (pgs. 191-192)

13. meditating; THE BLESSING (pg. 192)

14. faith; Garden of Eden (pg. 194)

15. Him (pg. 196)

16. ours; heirs; Garden (pg. 197)

17. Jesus; rest (pg. 198)

18. Garden of Eden; gospel; open (pg. 198)

19. You; You; You; You; I'll (pg. 200)

CHAPTER 11

The LORD and High Priest of
THE BLESSING

1. High Priest (pg. 205)

2. forgiveness; cleansing (pg. 205)

3. Lordship; high priesthood (pg. 208)

4. the Anointed One; His Anointing; Victor; Champion; Conquering King (pgs. 208-209)

5. delegated (pg. 210)

6. WORD; stand of faith (pg. 211)

7. Genesis; Hebrews; tithing (pg. 219)

8. faith (pg. 219)

9. blood; an oath (pg. 220)

10. anchored (pg. 221)

11. hard (pg. 226)

CHAPTER 12

Following the Faith of Abraham

1. born again (pg. 229)

2. joint heirs (pg. 229)

3. without faith (pg. 230)

4. family (pg. 232)

5. believe in Him (pg. 236)

6. WORD; lifestyle (pgs. 236-237)

7. Manufacturer's manual (pg. 237)

8. The WORD; final authority (pg. 238)

9. your attention (pg. 238)

10. The Buildup (pg. 240)

11. work; seed (pg. 240)

12. spirit; faith (pg. 241)

13. words (pg. 242)

14. speak; words of faith; act (pgs. 245-246)

15. imitator; to mimic (pg. 245)

16. 2 Kings 4; The Shunammite woman (pg. 247)

17. believed (pg. 248)

18. Delivery; declaration of faith; victory (pg. 251)

19. faith (pg. 253)

20. 10 years (pg. 254)

21. hope; faith (pg. 260)

CHAPTER 13

Breaking the Fear Connection

1. tolerated; contaminated (pg. 266)

2. faith (pg. 269)

3. curse (pg. 270)

4. anointing (pg. 271)

5. faith in Jesus; fear (pgs. 271, 276)

6. The power of love (pg. 279)

7. we are loved by God (pg. 279)

8. right; The WORD (pg. 285)

CHAPTER 14

The Royal Law of the Kingdom

1. love (pg. 293)

2. THE BLESSING (pg. 294)

3. nerves; cells (pg. 298)

4. peace (pg. 310)

5. forgiveness (pg. 316)

6. God; activate; love; commandment of love (pg. 320)

7. time with The LORD; daily (pg. 322)

8. covenant (pg. 323)

9. Garden of Eden; wealth (pg. 325)

CHAPTER 15

Come Sit With Me

1. We (pg. 330)

2. Hebrews (pg. 331)

3. THE BLESSING (pg. 350)

4. The WORD; Faith talks (pg. 354)

5. THE BLESSING; Abraham; Christ Jesus (pg. 359)